A BRIGHTER WITNESS

A BRIGHTER WITNESS

DWIGHT GUSTAFSON

CONVERSATIONS *on the* CHRISTIAN *and the* ARTS

journeyforth®

Greenville, South Carolina

Library of Congress Cataloging-in Publication Data

Gustafson, Dwight.
  A brighter witness : conversations on the Christian and the arts / Dwight Gustafson.
      p. cm.
    Summary: "Essays on the Christian and the Arts"—Provided by publisher.
    ISBN 978-1-60682-051-3 (perfect bound pbk. : alk. paper) — ISBN 978-1-60682-097-1 (e-book) 1. Christianity and the arts. I. Title.
  BR115.A8G87 2013
  261.5'7—dc23
                                                                    2012027219

All Scripture is quoted from the Authorized King James Version.

Cover design by Craig Oesterling
Page layout by Michael Boone

© 2013 by BJU Press
Greenville, South Carolina 29614
JourneyForth Books is a division of BJU Press

Printed in the United States of America
All rights reserved

ISBN 978-1-60682-051-3
eISBN 978-1-60682 -097-1

15 14 13 12 11 10 9 8 7 6 5 4 3 2 1

*To Gwen,
who brought God's beautiful Song
into my life*

CONTENTS

Preface   ix

Acknowledgments   xi

Introduction
   Drawing   3

The Witness of Art
   A Brighter Witness   9
   Behold the Lamb of God   13
   Sometimes a Light Surprises   16
   No Melody   20
   Ensemble   24
   Echoes   27
   Intermission   31

The Witness through Art
   His Career and the Rescue Mission   37
   My Family and the Rescue Mission   41
   Caroling   43
   Our Best   47

The Unflawed Witness
   Music's Power   53
   Praising God   56
   Pleasing God   58
   Beauty and Holiness   61
   Benediction   64

Coda
   His Glory   69

   Photo credits   73

PREFACE

The arts are a noble, creative gift from God. But they can be self-consuming. Their jewel-like facets may glow slightly in the spotlight of recognition and praise. But for the Christian who lives only for the arts and a career, they will not reflect the sunshine brilliance of God's glory.

These little essays have been on my heart for some time. Although they draw illustrations from my nearly fifty years in Christian higher education as a dean, teacher, conductor, and composer, and also in the professional world of the arts, the life principles they emphasize are not just for those vocationally committed to the arts and to arts education. They are central for all of us who have trusted Christ as Savior. They are also facets of a brighter witness to those who view and hear our work who do not know our Lord as Savior.

I hope our time together will be like an interesting conversation in which we talk of the arts as they connect with life while touching on important spiritual issues. And not just in a high-serious way miles apart from where we live. The stories should take care of that. Their incidents have lived in my mind for many a year, and if I have done my work well they will live a while in others' also.

Some are recollections from a childhood shaped by godly parents alert to special interests and abilities emerging in the play of their small boy, aptitudes they could nurture in spiritual as well as artistic directions. Others draw from my years as a guide of European fine-arts tours sponsored by my university. Together they distill a half century of my life as an educator and a performer. They speak of things learned and proved, and worthy, I believe, of passing on.

                                Dwight Gustafson

ACKNOWLEDGMENTS

These essays began as several magazine articles, but when my friend and colleague Ron Horton read them, he urged me to keep going and write them into a short book. He then generously agreed to be my editor. His skills at writing and parsing the English language are well-known to his students and faculty colleagues here, and in the professional world as well. These essays in their present form bear the imprint of his exacting mind, and I am most grateful.

I owe a great debt to the more than one hundred faculty and production staff of the Bob Jones University School of Fine Arts, with whom I worked for over fifty years. Their professionalism was always of the highest order, but even more important was their dedication to their calling of God in the arts, a commitment that was the foundation of our work.

Authors almost always recognize their families. Most children know what their father does at work, but in this case my four saw it firsthand as members of orchestras, stage managers, soloists, and members of choirs, oratorio choruses, and opera casts. Our repartee around the family table often included favorite stories, from legendary opera soloists to hidden members of the stage crew. What a privilege it was for a musician father to actually work along with his children, but even better, to see them continue to use their talents as adults for the glory of God.

The prima donna, the legendary soprano, usually gets the last curtain call. I have conducted many of them. But in this case, the talent goes far beyond the stunning voice. My wife, Gwen, had that on stage, but most important, behind the scenes she supported her husband and children with steady patience and a constant attention to Christian character. Her keen intelligence and insight guided us all.

Musicians reading this will understand the pressures of rehearsal and performance. Some will be fortunate enough to have this kind of loving spiritual hand at their side.

INTRODUCTION

DRAWING

If you look for the word "draw" in your dictionary you will find a long, exhausting paragraph of entries. I will consider only two, and they are familiar to us all. Drawing can mean "to make a sketch." It can also mean "to cause to move after or toward one by applying continuous force." Both meanings apply in this narrative. They are the bookends of this Christian's journey through life.

As a very young boy, without any prodding or contact with the arts, I became fascinated with drawing. Lying on the living room rug next to the cabinet radio with pencil and paper at hand and listening to melodramas (*The Lone Ranger*, *Jack Armstrong*, *The Shadow*, and more), I sketched what I saw in my imagination as the fifteen-minute segments played out. The same was true for football games. No video, just an excited announcer was inspiration enough for drawing players in various dramatic poses. Only recently have I realized that I had available first-quality artist sketch pads, not the thin yellow paper my own children used by the ream in their "coloring phase." My mother saw more in what I was doing than a "coloring phase."

I was allowed to draw in church. I must have been very young. Our whole family sat in the second pew from the front. One Sunday we had a visiting Scottish preacher: black frock coat, white starched high collar, and beautiful silk tie (it really was a cravat). My inspiration was not his sermon but his appearance. To me he looked like a penguin. That is what I sketched, plus a rather good likeness of his face. After the service ended I showed the sketch to my mother. She thought it was hilarious and went to show it to the preacher's wife. Evidently the lady did not agree with my mother's evaluation, and an unhappy scene ensued. Thus ended my drawing in church. But even the spilling of a bottle of India ink on the living room rug did not dissuade my mother's support. My sketching went on at home.

Throughout high school I took all the art courses offered, plus lessons at a private school for talented teens. Art was the major chosen for college. The University was one of only two genuinely Christian schools in the United States that had viable art programs. I was in my element, but I began to hear the same call of the Holy Spirit that I had heard in high school. The Lord was calling me to full-time Christian service. He was gently drawing me with His cords of love. Opportunities in music began to multiply, and in the spring I told the Lord I would follow His will.

At that point all signs pointed to a ministry in church music. I changed to a major in music as a sophomore. The path that followed is a long story that some readers will know. But the point here is that a loving God, seeing the self-willed struggles of a young boy, drew him to a place where he clearly saw God's will and opportunities for service, and he obeyed. It was a decision that would lead him down paths he could not imagine.

I have only a few memories of my childhood, but one is distinct. My middle name is Leonard, after my father, whose original, legal name was the Swedish "Lennart." I clearly remember that several times our pastor stopped and patted me on the head and said, "Dwight L. . . . Dwight L. Moody." Perhaps that was the seed for future thoughts about Christian work. Despite the tough times after World War II, my parents agreed to pay for my entire freshman year at the university. But they had one stipulation: because I had been doing a good deal of singing, I should take voice lessons. Years later, after I was well settled into my college ministry, they told me they had hoped and prayed God would lead me into full-time Christian work. I certainly would be no Dwight L. Moody, but I do know that "the effectual fervent prayer of a righteous man availeth much."

As I ponder God's leading, the words of an old gospel song come to mind. My father often chose it when he led congregational singing.

> I've found a Friend, O such a Friend!
> He loved me ere I knew Him:
> He drew me with the cords of love,
> And thus He bound me to Him.
>
> James Small, 1817–1888

In my work in the arts with college and high school students through the years, that decision, my surrender, has remained fresh and vital. It has spurred me to help lead them, with God doing the drawing, to that same vital decision in their lives.

THE WITNESS
OF ART

A BRIGHTER WITNESS

The European study tours in art and music that I conducted every three years for students and other adults often began in Belgium. St. Bavo Cathedral in Ghent, Belgium, is not on the itinerary of a typical fifteen-day European tour. Nearby Brussels and Bruges have dozens of interesting sights for the first-time tourist. However, in the seventies and eighties St. Bavo was on our list for two reasons. First, it housed what many consider to be the greatest Northern European Renaissance painting in existence. Second, this masterpiece was still located in the place for which it was painted.

In our day a painting is usually exhibited in a professional gallery along with other paintings. Today's artist relies on the gallery to sell it. But in earlier times most works were produced on commission for a specific place. They had a reason to be in that space, not like hundreds of works in a museum today vying for our attention. I am for museums. They have made possible the saving of the past for our eyes. But it is wonderful to see a great work in its own setting such as, in the church of the Frari in Venice, the Bellini altarpiece in the chapel and the Titian "Assumption" hanging over the main altar. But now come with me to St. Bavo.

This is the seventies, so there are rarely long tourist lines in Europe. It is time for the public elementary schools to be out, and local guides throughout Belgium are bracing themselves for the clusters of chattering children and energetic teachers who will soon be descending upon them. Fortunately we have come early enough so that these clusters of students are few.

One large group is just leaving the cathedral. We enter an almost empty church. It is not among the great churches, not highly decorated. In fact, our guide does not go down the center aisle but moves immediately to the right side aisle. The side aisles on left and right in these large churches are where the donations of the wealthy and powerful have provided small individual chapels, some completely open, a few closed or barred and restricted to private worship.

We arrive at a simple paneled cubicle, and an attendant waits at its door and gestures to us to come in. It is not large. Our group of thirty or so fills its interior comfortably. All its walls are dark wood. The only decoration is the huge altarpiece that fills the entire left wall. The sudden splendor of its eight exterior panels is startling, even for those who have no artistic bent. In 1432 Hubert and Jan Van Eyck finished this great work on a commission from Ghent's mayor, Jodocus Vyd, and his wife. These two are kneeling in the left and right bottom panels.

This is "The Adoration of the Mystic Lamb." Its crystalline beauty and powerful subject matter drew throngs to see it, even in the early years after its creation. Orators stood beside it regularly to explain its great unfolding story to crowds of viewers. Many of them could not read.

The guide begins, and she is excellent. Now comes the moment when she opens the large panels. In the interior of the painting the splendor is multiplied. Twelve separate panels tell one story: paradise with the slain Lamb, God the Father, Mary, John the Baptist, Adam and Eve, apostles, saints, martyrs, singing angels, and more. All is rich with color and exquisite detail, all painted for this one small chapel. I have never seen an uninterested tour member here.

Her lecture ends, and she graciously asks me for further comments. Then she closes the outer panels, and our group begins to leave. Suddenly I wonder if I will ever see this marvel again, and I ask her to take the group on through the cathedral and I will meet them outside in about ten minutes.

10

Almost alone in this space, but with two wary attendants looking on, I again view the eight outer panels. They are rich in detail, somewhat darker than what they conceal. The artist has painted dark and light as distinct shadows across these panels to emphasize the natural light that comes from a window high and to the right.

I ask if I may open the panels again. The attendants understand my gestures and nod approvingly. My hands touch the two frames. My fingers are inches from John the Baptist and John the Evangelist. I carefully open the panels to see paradise once again, for just ten precious minutes.

The artists have deliberately flooded the interior scene with brilliant painted light. It is a marvelous composition, and I look for more detail—trees and plants, tapestries and jewels, armor and swords reflecting light. An angel in the upper right panel plays a portative organ, the fingers of her left hand pressing down precisely on three white keys, C, E, and G [see fig. 3]. There is so much to see in the particulars, and yet a marvelous whole.

There is one detail that I must find once more, so I move carefully until I am within inches of the surface, hands at my side so as not to alarm the guards. On the neckline of Mary's rich blue tapestry dress [see fig. 4], there is a decorative band that includes a broach with a rich red stone at its center. I look closely and almost touch the panel. On the broach I find it! In the upper right corner of that red stone, there it is—an exact miniature reflection of the window high on the outer wall to my right, whose natural light would reflect on a real polished stone. There is no question the altarpiece is in exactly the right place.

Years later we return expectantly only to find that a separate brick building of inconsequential architecture, standing to the left of the cathedral, is the new home for the altarpiece. Hordes of tourists had endangered the great work. Security is tight as we enter the darkened space. The twelve inner panels are flooded with artificial light. The light bounces off the plexiglass that now protects the painting. The outer panels have been removed to be on permanent display in the rear.

Somehow all twenty panels, no longer together, have lost their original purpose. They are works apart. It is as though an ancient monk has been plucked out of his cell, taken apart, and whisked through time into a modern, highly lighted museum case.

And in the little chapel in the cathedral? There is a full-sized, rather grainy black-and-white photograph of the original—no color, no reflecting jewels, just a sanitized copy of the masterpiece. It is an unfortunate necessity. The crowds have grown. A great masterpiece must be protected.

There is a lesson here. The God of the universe created our world and out of its soil created man. Like the Van Eycks' brushes that painted each detail of that great painting, God's brush painted our every detail before we entered the world. The Psalmist speaks of His subtle artistry. "For thou hast possessed my reins: thou hast covered me in my mother's womb. . . . My substance was not hid from thee, when I was made in secret. . . . Thine eyes did see my substance, . . . and in thy book all my members were written" (Psalm 139:13–16). God attended to every detail of each of our features with a skill unimaginably greater than that available to the greatest of human artists, and the painting can remind us of that.

But the story told by the painting is not the whole of the story. Lighted now by spotlights, the Van Eycks' painting is no longer in its rightful place and is the worse for it. It is no longer in that simple room where every day from dawn till dark that one high window sheds downward its natural light. Now there is no jeweled surface to reflect that light, only a colorless grainy photograph.

Having accepted God's Redemption, will we then accept our places in the will of God where His artistry in us can most brilliantly reflect His glory? Will the brighter witness be ours?

BEHOLD THE LAMB OF GOD

In 1515 an altarpiece for the chapel of an ancient hospital near Colmar, Germany, was completed by the architect-engineer-painter Matthias Grünewald. It was in three separate hinged layers. Like all such altarpieces it was to be opened in various positions for special days in the church calendar.

The two outer panels appear in almost every art history text, and with good reason. These panels have placed Grünewald as second only to Albrecht Durer among the artists of the German Renaissance. They portray the crucified Christ [see fig. 5] as no other panels have ever pictured Him. Why was this Crucifixion scene placed on the outside panels? Why, among the eight scenes of the altarpiece, was this scene chosen to be almost continuously visible? The answer takes us to the purpose of the altarpiece and directs our thoughts toward the highest function of art.

This chapel was part of an ancient hospital. We can picture the poor and sick, most of them illiterate, being carried or helped along, then standing mutely gazing on the powerful scene. Christ had suffered for them, suffered much more than they would ever suffer, but for their eternal Redemption. No text was needed. The message was certain. It shouted in the thick crown of thorns, the gruesome physical detail, the greenish tinge of the flesh, the torn legs and torso, the skewed, straight arms of His body in death that seem to pull the crosspiece down with them.

However, there were seven words, written for the few who could read. Just above the arm of John the Baptist, who stands at one side and points with outstretched arm at the cross and its victim, are John's words, "He must increase, but I must decrease."

The sick and weak saw that the Savior's loincloth was made of the same old, torn linen as their own bandages. On the ground beside pleading Mary Magdalene was the jar of precious ointment she had once poured over her Savior. Would some ointment heal their wounds? Strangely, this was a night scene, one of the first nocturnal Crucifixions painted. Anyone who has lain awake in a hospital bed late at night needs no further explanation.

When the panels are opened to the second layer, a burst of light is unleashed. At the left Mary humbly hears Gabriel's annunciation, and then in the center she smiles at her baby while a wonderful, glistening instrumental consort of angels serenades. But on the right is one of the most brilliant Resurrection scenes in all Renaissance painting. Christ is rising, completely encircled by a bright, glowing halo of light [see fig. 6]. Roman guards are falling and writhing in the darkness below.

Oh, that church calendars and traditions could have been swept aside so that this panel would have been opened often, not just on holy days. Then the sick and suffering would have seen ever before them God's great plan: the miracle of Christ's birth as God and Man, and then His ultimate victory as God and Man over sin and death.

A great twentieth-century symphony was inspired by this altarpiece. Paul Hindemith had wanted to write an opera based on Grünewald's life but had been unable to move the creative process to bring the opera to birth. After contemplating the painting, Hindemith began work on the libretto for his *Mathis der Mahler*. Work went slowly until Hindemith decided to write a prelude for each act based on a panel of the altarpiece. A symphony resulted and was an immediate success. Then the composition of the opera flowed freely.

Envisioning the outer panels of this altarpiece, one may hear, as I do, in a more familiar work, that G octave leap of Handel's altos as they begin the phrase "Behold the lamb of God." Then sopranos, then basses, and then tenors imitate the leap, drawing as it were our gaze up to the cross. The imitation continues—"that taketh away the sin of the world." And then these vocal lines converge in those slow, ponderous chords that seem to carry the burden of all sin that God's Son bears.

But now the panels open and we see the victorious, resurrected Christ. Hear that famous D Major chord from the orchestra. We breathe together and sing in affirmation, "Worthy is the lamb that was slain, and hath redeemed us to God by His blood, to receive power, and riches, and wisdom, and strength, and honor, and glory and blessing." Now unison tenors and basses more quickly proclaim, "Blessing and honor, glory and power be unto Him that sitteth upon the throne and unto the Lamb," and the entire chorus takes up the refrain, passing it back and forth.

Suddenly, three slashing eighth-note figures in the chorus, like giant timpani, announce the final cascading counterpoint of all the parts. Then an instant of silence, and the choir as a powerful chorale sings "forever and ever," with those powerful, compressed Handelian chords. But this is not the end, for the final chord of this chorale is a dominant that cries out for resolution. It comes as the basses begin the mighty, lengthy "Amen" fugue that echoes the "Amen" again and again through all the voices, affirming this great Redemption story.

Handel chose a mighty double fugue to end his masterpiece. It was no mere academic exercise. When performed with firmness and power, it crowns his great work like Grünewald's brilliant halo, displaying in luminous splendor the triumphant Redeemer and glorified Christ.

SOMETIMES A LIGHT SURPRISES

The student tour had come to Salzburg, and my mother was with my wife and me. She had recently become a widow. It was a difficult time for her, but the tour was like a tonic. The three of us had many hours together, including some private ones. But she also greatly enjoyed the testimony and jovial camaraderie of the university students. From my experience now as an "older person," I know just how she felt. Being able to continue my work with students has been a privilege and a great joy.

It was a warm afternoon. I had always wanted to see and experience the Mozarteum, one of the world's great conservatories. It attracts the most talented student musicians from around the world. The timing of past visits had never worked out. We had never entered it, not even its concert hall, with its list of past performers that reads like a "who's who" of music. It was summer, and I knew from posted schedules that it was not "in session."

Let's try to get in anyway! We took a short walk and stood there before the empty, silent building. No sound of music, but we went to the door. It was unlocked! We stepped into an empty hall, but then heard footsteps. A short, jovial janitor appeared, looking almost like the Sacristan in Puccini's *Tosca*. I thought we would be ushered out. But he spoke a little English and asked if we would like to see more. Would we! Well of course, especially the concert hall. Our private tour began.

I stood at the back of the beautiful hall and could almost imagine the sound. Perhaps it was three world-class musicians finishing the last movement of the Mendelssohn Piano Trio No. 2 with its quotation of the great hymn tune "Old Hundredth,"

Dwight Gustafson

or Orpheus, the touring American chamber orchestra, playing the grand fugue that ends Mozart's Jupiter Symphony. But alas, all was silent. I took some shillings from my pocket and with words of much gratitude placed them in the open, welcoming hand of the janitor.

But then, with a twinkle in his eye he said, "Do you want to see the Magic Flute House?" I was astounded! I had forgotten that this tiny, cabin-like structure had been moved from its original location in Vienna to the "backyard" of the Mozarteum. The negotiations for its moving must have been intense.

We walked across the grass. Our guide unlocked the door. We entered. And there we were, in the small room where Mozart, as usual with lightning speed, had written the opera that has charmed young and old for over two hundred years. We carefully examined the simple room. It had never been on any tour brochure I had ever seen. Only musicians can understand the joy we felt. This was not a large museum with a painting looted hundreds of years earlier from some monastery and a lecture from a kind but tired guide. This was a real place that still existed in real time.

Those of you who have had the opportunity to travel extensively will know such things. When the good memories of your touring come to mind, you almost instantly remember these wonderful, unplanned moments. They happen only once. They can never be duplicated. But you were there!

Though an Almighty God knows everything—past, present, and future—He doesn't reveal our earthly future to us during our Christian walk. But in His providence He reserves a few wonderful, unplanned moments to encourage us, to remind us of His faithfulness and loving care. We all have had them. There were those other times we persevered in prayer, wondering if we would ever see God's hand, God's answer, and then in time, perhaps a very long time, the answer graciously came. But there were also those unexpected moments, dramatic intersections of ordinary life that glowed like candles in the dark, when God's guidance was suddenly revealed. The visit to the Mozarteum was one. Here is another one, just a few weeks old as I write.

The opportunity to write a three-movement piece for choir and orchestra was in place. The Psalms were my first choice for text. The middle movement, which would be quiet and reflective, required that sort of text. Psalm 34 caught my attention. Verse eight jumped out at me, because it was the text for a simple but beautiful motet, written by the English composer Ralph Vaughan Williams for the coronation of Elizabeth II. My choirs had done it several times. "O taste and see that the Lord is good; blessed is the man that trusteth in him." The melody took shape, and I changed "good" to "gracious" because it sang better. Vaughan Williams had done the same. I also altered the next phrases. In my defense, fine composers and poets since Calvin have been slightly altering Psalm texts to make them sing better.

The piece needed dramatic contrast. Verses six and seven were ideal, especially verse six. "This poor man cried, and the Lord heard him, and saved him out of all his trouble." At this point a plan took shape. Each of the three movements would be dedicated to the memory of a colleague and friend who had gone to be with the Lord. This was to be Joan Mulfinger's piece. A widow, she had finished raising the nine of her eleven children who were still at home when their father, George, a brilliant science professor and fine musician himself, died of cancer. They were our neighbors. Joan was a superb violinist with a forty-two-year teaching career; but best of all, she had a child-like faith that put us all to shame. A violin solo in the piece would be my special memorial to her.

After the concert four of the children, all married women, were in line to greet me. They were obviously deeply moved. One said that I must have done research because I used their dad's verse. The next morning, realizing that I didn't know the whole story, I phoned one of the girls. She told me that the verse in the middle, verse six, was the one her dad had chosen as God's message for him when he learned he had cancer.

I had not known that! But God knew it, and He placed it there in the piece. We cannot know the mind of God, but this seemed to be a divine exclamation point, telling this composer that the full story needed to be told, and that only God could tell it in exactly the right way.

> Sometimes a light surprises
> The Christian while he sings;
> It is the Lord who rises
> With healing in His wings:
> When comforts are declining,
> He grants the soul again
> A season of clear shining,
> To cheer it after rain.
>
> William Cowper, 1731–1800

NO MELODY

If you have children or grandchildren who are taking music lessons and it's time for the annual recital, you know well that nervous feeling in the pit of your stomach as your young musician walks on stage to perform. A small dose of pride, if such is allowable for parents and grandparents, may help to alleviate those symptoms. If that child becomes a successful musician, your anxiety will lessen.

Still anything can happen at a recital and not uncommonly does. With professionals the chances of a mishap are fewer but still possible. That nervous feeling you had as you waited for your child to step onstage has now passed to the accomplished performer himself as he waits backstage thinking through his checklist and hoping and praying that all is ready. Believe me, I have stood beside many a nervous professional backstage, even world-class performers. Anything can happen. We always hope it doesn't.

Still there are those times, and I'll tell you of one of them. We were sitting, all 250 tourists, on the individual gilded chairs with red-velvet upholstery that fill what is called the "marble room" in the Mirabell Palace in Salzburg, Austria [see fig. 7]. A marble room it is . . . or at least seems. Floor, walls, and ceiling, though plaster, are painted cleverly to look like marble. That was the style in eighteenth-century Austria. It was a palace fit for a king. But the ruler of the town, the archbishop, actually resided in a fortress castle across the Salz river on the high hill that overlooks the city. Mirabell Palace, this more secluded spot, was built for his mistress. Enough said about the archbishop's life style.

However, this was the room in which one evening a tiny young boy and his sister, accompanied by their doting but determined father, played a command performance for the archbishop. In later years that boy, now a young man, would write and perform a new mass almost every week for the impatient bishop-ruler. Who were his family? Their name was Mozart. What history is embedded in these walls!

This night two talented young Austrians, a female violinist and a male pianist, were playing. Palace concerts are performed every night from late spring into August. They provide an opportunity for young professionals to take that next step into a larger career, if all goes well.

Alas, a potential disaster occurred. As the music rose beautifully to a fever pitch and during a sweeping up-bow, the woman lost her hold on the bow. It sailed like an arrow high in the air over her shoulder, descended, and slammed on the floor.

There followed a discreet, subdued laughter from the audience. She was a good sport. She smiled and walked over to retrieve her bow. Most who amusedly watched this javelin throw would not have known that the bow was probably much more expensive per inch than the violin. The bow is to the violin what breath is to a singer. Without a doubt she would have had a spare, inexpensive bow in her violin case backstage, but it would not perform nearly as well as the "fallen arrow."

I held my breath as she carefully looked it over, felt the hairs at the tip and at the handle, which is called the frog. Talk about a nervous stomach! Had the bow been crippled? Would it survive the concert?

She slowly loosened and then retightened it. For the young lady those few minutes of silence must have seemed like an eternity. Were a good press review and a career hanging in the balance? She started to play, and I held my breath. Then all was well. The melody was full and rich. There was a sigh almost in unison as the audience relaxed.

A few minutes later disaster struck again! A string in the Bechstein grand piano suddenly broke, with a loud snap. The concert stopped again. The young pianist rose and worked inside the piano, trying to tie back loose ends so the performance could continue. He then sat down, and on they played.

Mercifully the official intermission soon came, and they left the room. In just a few minutes out came a piano technician, probably summoned from his living-room chair elsewhere in town. He busied himself inside the piano, tying the offending remains of the string safely out of the way. Why not a new string? Out of the question. In its upper range a grand piano has three strings for each pitch. Together they balance volume and resonance with the single large strings in the bass. A new string would take thirty minutes to install and tune. Then in its newly strained state, it would go quickly out of tune with its partners. The young musicians gamely finished their recital.

Everything had been in place: a talented, dynamic young performer, her expensive violin, an expert accompanist, an expectant and sympathetic audience, a "marble room" that reflected sound like a giant bathroom shower, and the possibility of another professional success. But without the bow for the violin, there could be no recital. Without replacement of the string the recital could go on but not so well.

There is no such thing as a perfect performance, just as there is no such thing as a perfect Christian life. But we who have trusted Christ as Savior now have a trustworthy, ever-present friend, the third person of the Trinity, the Holy Spirit. He is ever with us to encourage, to guide, to correct, and to convict. We can ignore His presence, but like the missing bow or a bow locked up in our violin case, the melody of His presence and guidance is absent. Our life, the instrument, still has its potential, but silence tells it all. The Holy Spirit's matchless melody is missing.

Or we can be like the beleaguered pianist who plays on with one broken, silent string. We can hobble on, hoping that the remaining two strings will sound something like the original three; but we know the difference. We know that the Spirit has been hindered. And sometimes our family and friends know it as well.

A Christian may play a fine performance on stage and enjoy the applause. But the real performance, his walk with God, is just hobbling along when that broken string could be replaced and tuned.

At this point we could stop and have a theological discussion about the Holy Spirit. That might gratify our minds, not satisfy our souls. Rather, I suggest that in the next few quiet moments we pray the beautiful prayer poem written by George Croly more than one hundred years ago. It tells God, much better than we can say it, of our desire to experience the work of His Spirit in our lives.

> Spirit of God, descend upon my heart;
> Wean it from earth, through all its pulses move;
> Stoop to my weakness, mighty as Thou art,
> And make me love Thee as I ought to love.
>
> George Croly, 1780–1860

ENSEMBLE

The American Heritage Dictionary defines "ensemble" in music as "a unit or group of complementary parts that contribute to a single effect." How does this singleness of effect happen among performing musicians concentrating to achieve it? How do they bring it off? Look now at an orchestra with all those difficult, varying instruments and one conductor somehow managing to hold it together.

I must reveal a secret. Orchestra members may tell you what they have heard, couching it carefully, that an orchestra is a democracy run by a dictator. This expression does in fact, though with a little exaggeration, describe an orchestra if all is going well.

Still, how do ninety professional musicians concentrate so that they all sound together exactly at the same time as the conductor's beat hits its "ictus" or attack? Do they wait for his "swoop"? Do they all have the precise subdivision of that gliding movement of the baton placed in each of their brains so as to react at the identical time?

You may remember seeing and hearing a great orchestra perform and recall your discomfort when the conductor gave a clear, precise beat and there was a microsecond pause. Yes, all ninety musicians played absolutely together, but their attack came "a hair" after his beat. You were not just imagining. Not all orchestras and conductors perform this way, but some do. It is a German-European style of conducting that is favored by some for its effect on the sound and response of the orchestra. But how is it done?

Stranger yet, there is a world-famous chamber orchestra, Orpheus, less than half the size of the New York Philharmonic, that both performs and records with no conductor. In fact within a single concert its string players will change places for each piece. And what might be the explanation for all this? Ensemble.

The first step in the ensemble process is accountability. If you are hired to play in the Metropolitan Opera Orchestra as seventh out of eight second violins and you go to your first rehearsal of Verdi's *Don Carlo,* everyone there, including the conductor, James Levine, will already know the music thoroughly. You had better know yours. All rests on thorough preparation. If this step hasn't been taken, there will be no more steps. You will learn the hard way about accountability.

Fine musicians who thoroughly know the music do follow each other. They follow in the sense that they think and watch and respond to each other with a precise agreement on matters of attack, tempo, style, expression, and their own place among the players in the orchestra. You can see something of the same thing in action on TV on Monday night football. Not ninety, not thirty, but eleven men on the field whose minds, bodies, spirit, and understanding are attempting to work precisely together to win the game. The quarterback will be the hero or the goat because he is the one placed in charge. He will be considered responsible for the good or bad playing of the team and its individual members.

But in excellent music, what makes for ensemble? Even with a fine, dynamic leader, the visual, aural, and body-language messages are constantly flying back and forth between the conductor and players and among the players. Messages are constantly being received and responded to and are being thoroughly enjoyed by players and audience in a great performance.

For example, the key first chair of each section of strings is their leader. He or she is encouraging his or her comrades as a jockey would encourage his horse at the Kentucky Derby. At the same time, these four section leaders are watching, listening, and working together as if they were a single string quartet. The wind players are blending with each other and at the same time attacking and blending with strings and brass. Percussionists are poised to place sound precisely where required. The result is a beautiful unity of expression and style that even the untrained listener will hear and feel.

Every musician reading this account will remember those performances when such a thing happened. They were glorious. And who was responsible? The conductor? Most certainly. There must be a dynamic leader for large forces. But success is ultimately with the ensemble spirit of conductor and players.

Ensemble is not a concept restricted to music. The Orpheus chamber orchestra does demonstrations of its techniques in management seminars for men and women who are not musicians. Management has discovered something here. Ensemble works in business as well as music. It is a universal principle of success.

As believers, have we discovered it? We have a God-inspired, detailed explanation of ensemble for the body of believers. Romans and other Epistles are replete with clear directions and encouragement about the cooperation of pastor and members, brother with brother, believers corporately with individual members.

A musician feels and enjoys all of the responsibility described above and creates something of high value in doing so. But for the Christian, ensemble has eternal consequences. Had Bible-based, heartfelt, spiritual ensemble been a priority with pastors, elders, deacons, staff members, and congregation, how many church ministries would have flourished and not been wounded or broken? How many valuable works for God would have been saved? How many Christian friendships would have flourished instead of decaying? How many lost souls would have come to Christ in a service or quietly prayed with a friend at a coffee-shop table? How many thirsting souls would have been struck with wonder and desire as they saw the love of Christ shed abroad?

ECHOES

It was a beautiful summer evening, just after dusk. The boat was gliding through the mirror-like waters of Switzerland's Lake Lucerne, and my study tour group was enjoying the calm after a busy day. We had spent the morning on Mount Pilatus and the afternoon shopping and sightseeing in the town of Lucerne.

We were seated along with other tourists in the large, single cabin of the "Night Boat," eating rather ordinary cheese fondue but thoroughly enjoying the colorful costumes and folk music of a band of local musicians. One young man played the alpine horn. It is about twelve feet long, made of wood with no holes or valves. It depends on the practiced lips of the player to change the pitches. It is in this respect much like a bugle but with a full, rich sound. He offered it to volunteers, and I took a try at it; but at my lips it sounded more like a car horn. The group applauded my ungainly "premiere." Then the performers invited us all to come upstairs to the rear deck.

In the darkness the boat moved slowly toward steep rocky cliffs that dropped almost straight into the water. When we were within a few feet of the cliffs the boat stopped. The motor was turned off, and all lights were extinguished. The lights of the town of Lucerne twinkled in the distance. For us Americans it was like a still, dark night in the country. The young man stepped toward the rail, set the large bowl of the horn's end on the deck, took hold of the middle of the instrument, pursed his lips, and blew softly and easily.

How I wished that all the student horn players I had ever worked with could have been there for that magic moment. The notes were clean and relaxed, yet rich and robust. The player's beautiful but simple "call" with its long notes and shorter-note embellishments went forth from the mountainside. But the magic? The magic was in the one, then two, then three, and then four echoing "calls" that seemed to come from as many mountainsides miles and miles away.

He played several times, but we wanted more. He played again and again, improvising new signals to imaginary herdsmen miles and miles away. It all comes back to my mind even now. But what especially took hold of my mind then and does so still? It was not the player, not the solo, but the total effect—yes, those beautiful, arching calls, but also and especially the magic of echoes that receded with enhancement, each softer but even more beautiful than the one before.

For the first time I believe I heard what some Austrian and German composers of the nineteenth and early twentieth century must have imagined when they were composing. They had traveled the Alps. This was a real-life sound for them. You hear those Swiss horns when you hear the four horns in Richard Strauss's *Don Juan* begin their unison line with that majestic octave leap. You hear it again when the solo horn of Wagner's *Siegfried* sounds across the stage from the orchestra pit. You hear it still again in the brilliant horn ensemble of the "Hunter's Chorus" in *Der Freischutz*. The list could go on and on.

But for me, the most beautiful mountain horn sound of all occurs at the end of the introduction to the last movement of Brahms's First Symphony. A sforzando chord leaves hushed low strings and timpani in place, and above this a French horn plays two majestic "calls." A second horn enters on the last note of each "call," subtly sustaining the line. Then two flutes, like two high wisps of clouds, echo the "calls," and trombones and low winds play a short chorale. Next, like our lake boat alpine-horn player, the solo horn calls twice again. But this time the second horn echoes the calls a half step higher. Then the orchestra cadences, and that great C Major melody begins with violins playing its first resonant G on their open G string. You could well argue that the horns are just the anticipation. But what an anticipation! We have been held in its power.

A thought struck me then which has stayed with me since—that our lives can be like the alpine horn. We can initiate the call, but we can only listen as God directs the echoes. We may not realize at the time that we are calling. One afternoon I was walking back to my office from the Student Center and was almost in front of the art gallery, when a young man approached and asked if we could talk. We certainly could. He told me he was almost at the same spot on the sidewalk one night, returning to his room after work at the dining hall, when he saw me and my daughter, a young university student, coming out the side door of the recital hall. She held her violin case, and I had my arm around her as we walked and talked. An orchestra rehearsal had ended, and we were going to my car.

He told me he had come from a broken home. He had not known the love he saw that night. Right there he had determined that with God leading he would marry a Christian girl and experience that kind of love. He would have a Christian family. What an echo!

Of course I could claim no credit. I was just a dad enjoying fellowship with a daughter I admired and loved dearly. God had wanted to encourage that young man, so He put us on that sidewalk at just the right time.

By the next day my thoughts had turned from the joy of being an encouragement to that discouraged young man to the realization that I was not worthy to be an example for God. He certainly knew my weaknesses and knew the times when I might not have been an "example of the believer." The incident opened my eyes again to the wonderful grace of God. Despite our weaknesses, God sees fit to use us for His glory.

Looking back, beyond praying for him I wish I had taken his name and asked him to keep in touch. So I will likely never know in this life if he did marry a fine Christian girl, if there are children, and if he has been a God-honoring husband and father. At the time of this writing he would be in his forties or

A Brighter Witness

older. One of his children could have been a student here, might even have been in some group I conducted. It would have been wonderful to hear some of the echoes.

And why say "some"? Because the echoes keep calling and calling and calling.

INTERMISSION

I had just returned to campus after doctoral study, and the symphony organization at the state capital asked me to write a piece for them. "Prelude for Strings and Harp" had its premiere, and, of course, Gwen and I were there with seats midway back in the auditorium. My piece was programmed just before intermission. There also was a short biographical sketch in the program. In the row right behind us an all-knowing lady evidently saw my bio and began to describe quite loudly and expansively to her friends all sorts of interesting things about the University. She was not being unkind, but we sat stunned and silent. Everything she was saying was dramatically far from the truth. Her unique narrative went on until the lights dimmed.

The "Prelude for Strings" got quite a good performance. The audience applauded. The conductor bowed and signaled the orchestra to stand. Then, as is the procedure in most premieres, the conductor looked to the center of the hall and with a gesture signaled to me, and I stood. More applause. The applause died, and the lights came up. When Gwen and I turned to go to the lobby, the half dozen or so seats behind us were already empty. The intermission was a refreshing break for us. When we returned to our seats, those seats were still empty. Obviously the intermission, for the lady and her friends, was a merciful chance to escape!

Aida was my first opera-conducting assignment—given me at the ripe old age of twenty-five. That memorable performance started well—for an instant, that is. The quiet prelude began. Muted first violins softly played the beautiful E-string love motif, and the second violins entered with their hushed counterpoint.

But the spell was broken as the top of a music stand pulled loose and crashed to the floor. There went the ethereal pianissimos!

The audience could not have noticed the second mishap. When the great triumphal scene began, the lights in my conductor's podium went out. For most of that scene, with its ranks of Egyptian soldiers, conquered Ethiopians, priests, townspeople, and four guest artists, I went by mind and not by sight. And what was the lesson to be learned? In opera, memorize, be ready for anything, *and* replace that ancient set of lights in advance. Great purposes can hang on the small business of life.

That was literally true in the next incident. The Brahms *Requiem* is among the great sacred works for chorus and orchestra. In the cavernous auditorium, two hundred singers, including all the choirs and all the voice students, were on stage. The orchestra pit was slightly lowered. Caution: if you are ever standing before an audience and wearing a "tails" outfit, be sure all buttons, clasps, and latches are secure. I never knew when in the music it happened, but suddenly I realized that the narrow left band, one of two that secured my white vest at my neck, had broken loose and was dangling like a white handkerchief down the left front of my coat. Then the right band similarly appeared. A button had broken!

The music and I swept on, and more and more of the two pieces that formed the vest folded down in front like two sails in the wind. At this point the chorus members were doing their best to hold steady at looking pleasant. The audience could see the chorus and orchestra but could not see my dilemma. When the entire vest was at my waist like a chef's apron, the chorus could hardly contain their strange, new-found joy. With at least thirty minutes to go, I knew they could not make it. I desperately grabbed the "apron" with my left hand, pulled suddenly and hard (in time, of course), and thankfully, the pieces of vest fell to the floor. I did not dare to look at the chorus, but after a few seconds the electricity seemed to subside. I looked up and regained contact, and we, like the vest, sailed on.

Dwight Gustafson

A dear friend of ours with her friend, both from Albany, New York, were our guests for the annual opera and were staying for a few days afterward. The opera was a first for the friend. As we often did after a performance, the family and others involved in the production gathered at our home for dessert and fellowship. Our guests joined us. My wife tells that the lady was quite overcome at being in the company of the "maestro's" family at the opera, and then being in his home after the performance. As always, I was the last to get home. I am told that in the interim in the pre-dessert conversation the dear lady kept referring to the "maestro" in a most fervent manner.

When I arrived, the accolades for the "maestro" continued. My family and I were amused but increasingly uncomfortable—that is, until my wife came up with a solution. As the table was being cleared and the usual kitchen chores began, she said, "Maestro, would you please take out the garbage?" There followed a moment of silence. Then the dear lady began to laugh and laugh, and so did we, as I did what I was told. Part of the small business of life on which great purposes can hang is not taking oneself too seriously.

THE WITNESS THROUGH ART

HIS CAREER AND THE RESCUE MISSION

I have seen young Christian artists whose gifts led them toward questionable opportunities. A young tenor who sang *Rigoletto*'s Duke with our University orchestra and singers was offered a contract by the New York City Opera. When he arrived there, his first assignment was Narraboth in Richard Strauss's *Salome*. The nature of the production grieved his spirit. He said he could not sing in it—a brave, biblical decision. He was dismissed, and his quest for bigger things ended.

There was also a young, very talented bass, with a voice like the boom of a large church bell, who by his late twenties was already among the world's great operatic basses, both in singing and acting. He began privately composing an opera based on the life of Christ. His intense study of the Scriptures for the project was the beginning of a long spiritual journey, an intellectual endeavoring to find peace with God. When in London on business, he heard a Salvation Army band playing in Hyde Park. It reminded him of an unkept promise made years earlier to sing for the army in New York.

He had first been attracted to ministries in the slums as background experience for his opera. This time he was in spiritual turmoil. He found the address of a Salvation Army Goodwill Center in the phone book and proceeded on foot into the London slums to find it. He began work as a volunteer on a truck collecting used items for resale, washing dishes in the center's kitchen, and finally singing in a service where a compelling gospel message was preached. He was among people whose lives were entirely different from anything he had experienced.

His amazing spiritual journey then took him to Detroit. Staying in a hotel just outside the slums, he again walked into skid row to find what he had experienced in London. His journey ended in the superintendent's office of the Detroit Rescue Mission. There Jerome Hines learned that Christ had atoned for his sins, and he accepted Him as his Savior.

From that moment on, Jerome Hines radiated his Savior. He had already been through the professional scramble from which the young tenor had withdrawn. For some reason, God wanted him to be a saint in Caesar's household.

Jerome Hines now seemed to control the wheel of his career. But God's plans are not always our plans. In the middle of it all he began to have vocal problems. I learned of it only when, in the middle of a solo concert at the University, he stopped and quietly announced to the audience that he was having vocal difficulties, would have to stop, but would return later to fulfill his obligation. The stunned audience was silent. The houselights came up, and the whispering, puzzled crowd left the hall. After a time he did return successfully to the opera stage, and his career continued.

Several years later on a Saturday morning, a small group of our ministerial students were on the streets of the state capital, giving out tracts and doing personal witnessing, when a tall imposing man came toward them. He asked what they were doing. They told him, and then Jerome Hines asked to join them, assisted with the tract distribution, and took them to lunch. He had been rehearsing that morning with the city symphony for that evening's concert.

When he came back to us to fulfill his obligation, it was then I got to know him. He and a Russian tenor friend did an all-Russian concert with the University orchestra and combined choirs. The first half consisted of Russian opera arias plus orchestral pieces. The second half was a costumed, semistaged performance of the coronation scene, the polonaise, and the clock scene from *Boris Godunov*. His memento for me was a large dramatic poster by the noted American poster artist LeRoy Neiman showing Hines as the fierce Boris. He had signed it for me and added the Scripture reference John 17:3: "And this is life eternal, that they might know thee the only true God, and Jesus Christ, whom thou hast sent."

Here is the point. In all his years, the rescue mission never left his life. When I asked about him, professionals always spoke respectfully about his testimony, what some would call his "sincere religious approach." One opera singer who had gone through many trials and had trusted Christ after he left the Met told me that he had sought out Hines for counsel and that it was part of the seed sown that eventually brought him to Christ. Only God knows how many lives Jerry's testimony touched.

Some would say, "He was converted at the top and didn't have to battle with decisions that lesser artists had to make." Not so. When still at the top of his career he went to the Met's general manager and asked to be excused from a production of *Faust* that he felt was inconsistent with his testimony. The request was granted, but he did not sing again at the Met for many years.

Jerry wrote and spent years reworking his own opera on the life of Christ, *I Am the Way*. With assistance from his professional colleagues it was produced several times throughout the U.S. and even in Russia. My last collaboration with him was his appearance with the University Opera Association in the title role of Boito's opera *Mefistofele*. He was scheduled for knee surgery a few weeks later. I noticed a hearing aid behind each ear that the audience wouldn't see. There would be no sweeping movements on stage. But his huge voice and dramatic persona carried the opera right along. I don't think anyone would have guessed his age. His last years were spent caring for an ailing wife who preceded him to Glory.

Some would say that the stage of Metropolitan Opera House and the altar rail of a Detroit rescue mission are worlds apart. Since Plato's time an idea has been afloat that life is divided between this real, in-your-face world and an elevated existence to which only the most talented and creative or the most morally astute occasionally rise. At this higher level one supposedly gains unmatched artistic insight or, in the case of nonartists, a broader moral vision than normal people have. Jerry did not live his life on two levels. I doubt an audition was required when he appeared for his first heavenly choir rehearsal. No doubt there were already singers in that choir who were there because his life was not just for Christ but *was* Christ. Within Jerome Hines the rescue mission was always alive.

That there are two levels of commitment in life is a dangerous idea for the Christian. Paul wrote under the inspiration of the Holy Spirit, "For to me to live is Christ" (Phil. 1:21). Every situation, every turn of the Christian's life, should be lived not just for Christ but *as* Christ.

MY FAMILY AND THE RESCUE MISSION

As a family, we were at the rescue mission quite often. Dad was an M.D., a meat dealer, who took every opportunity to preach.

The intricate part of getting ready to leave for the mission was loading the car. The biggest item was my mother's harp. There were no SUVs or vans in those days. A rear passenger door opened, and the harp was carefully moved into the car and then forward so that its base was propped over the front seat. The top or crown of the harp was then lifted and placed on the ledge under the car's back window.

Three children (my young brother was not yet on the team) got in the back seat, where there were two options. One could sit solo with the other two squeezed on the far side of the harp, or two could sit solo with the third crouched on the floor under the harp. Somehow my sister's cello was sometimes packed in too.

One night the men were waiting in the mission auditorium when we got there. (A meal at the mission means attendance at the evening service.) They got to see the preliminaries. The harp was placed on the platform and the cover was taken off. As usual, mother took her tuning key in one hand, deftly turning the tuning pins while her other hand played octaves. She finished the process with the usual flourish of ascending and descending chords that all harpists use, perhaps with more flourish than usual. There followed a moment of silence, and then the audience applauded. Who among them had ever seen, let alone heard, a live harp before!

These services were an early lesson for us children. You give back to God in service what He has given you, and you do it without regard for station and place. You do it when any door of opportunity, no matter how great or small, opens before you.

Jump ahead about thirty years with me. The director of the local rescue mission called me one night saying that a scheduled preacher had to cancel and could I come down? He had never heard me preach, but he had heard me sing at the mission. Of course, an invitation to me was an invitation to the family.

I was to preach, a University student was to play for the service, and my wife and I would sing a duet, "Savior like a Shepherd Lead Us." Why not use our youngest, though not quite a teen, as our accompanist? She had been taking piano for several years from a fine teacher. People at the mission do not expect an Artur Rubinstein, just someone to manage a simple four-part accompaniment. Expectations were not high—a reassuring thought, for as we entered the chapel I noticed that two blocks of wood inserted under the pedals were holding up the pedal assembly of the battered, old grand piano.

All was going well—for a while, that is. The University student was playing energetically as I led the congregation in the last hymn when suddenly the blocks slipped out and the whole pedal assembly crashed to the floor. The pianist, who had been relying too heavily on the pedal, was in musical shock. Now there was no pedal to make things connect and project.

Somehow we finished the song. But then must follow the duet. Our hearts were in our mouths as the little girl sat down at the piano. Then clearly, in four parts, with a fine legato connection she had learned well from her teacher, she played simply but beautifully, without pedal, the entire duet, interlude and all. When the service was over and the men had been counseled, I walked over to my daughter and said, "Welcome to Christian work!"

I draw from what happened this thought. Whether you are performing in Carnegie Hall or in the rescue mission, God deserves your very best—the best you can do with what you are given, in talent and in trying circumstances.

CAROLING

It is quiet on North 21st Street. The houses are silent. The ungainly Santa and reindeer next door seem out of place. Some decorative lights are shining their farewell for the season.

Any neighbor with a door or window cracked that afternoon would have heard the laughter when twenty or more adults and children were showing off presents in the big front room of the brick house. They would have heard a pianist play and a family begin to sing, and continue singing until the call to Christmas dinner.

Now the cars are gone, and the street is left to itself. The big front porch is dark. A few lights in the house are on, for two small girls and their mother remain in the living room. It looks as if Christmas is over for the year.

Change of scene. The second-floor Cardiac Unit at Arlington Hospital is quieter than usual. The small number of patients means less work. The staff has tried to get as many home for Christmas as possible. Only one nurse is out on rounds. The doctors have long since gone, and only a few family and visitors are with the remaining patients. Almost no one volunteers to work on Christmas night, and certainly the patients would rather be home. Even the poinsettias at the main nurses' station seem outdated. Nurses on the floor are in a thoughtful, quiet mood.

But then the elevator door down the hall opens. A dozen or more adults and children spill out into the hallway, laughing and talking. They assemble like a choir. A flute warms up, and copies of music are handed out. The tall, elderly gentleman, who must be the grandfather, gives instructions, raises his hands, and the sound of "Angels We Have Heard on High" fills the halls. They are singing all the parts! When the refrain arrives, basses are vying with sopranos to see how much ornamentation they can add to the lines.

This is no church choir—some are too young for that, or too old! It can't be a family, can it? The singers are too much at ease with all the musical details.

Then they move toward the nurses' station and the mood changes. The dark-haired girl who is serving as support for her grandmother is consulted. She thinks a moment, and then hums the pitch for "We Three Kings of Orient Are." Perfect pitch! The flute glides above the voices. Some nurses are smiling. Several are crying.

Could they go through the halls and sing for each of the patients? The answer is obvious, and they move silently to the first room. The man on the bed, though weak, has raised himself slightly; and his smile is one of wonderment and joy. No family, no visitors are here. He softly speaks. He is a choir director, and could he lead? Of course, and he can have whatever carol he chooses. "O Come All Ye Faithful" it is, and he is indeed a musician. Then he lies back on his bed with a contented smile and asks the group to bless him with one more.

We never learned the story of this man, old, alone, no family with him. As we begin "Joy to the World, the Lord Is Come" he nods his head in time to the music and relaxes on his bed. What Christmas choirs past had he heard in his mind today, there in his hospital room? What sights and sounds of better, brighter days had flooded his weary mind in the unusual stillness of that cardiac unit when he looked at his watch and saw it was the time for the family Christmas dinner—for the others to gather without him? We will never know.

I could go on to describe the delight and response of all the other patients. Those in one room were Spanish, but they obviously recognized the old melodies and some sang with us. But my mind keeps going back to that choir director. How he must have been amazed that in his loneliest hour, bereft of the joy of making Christmas music, suddenly God provided him with a choir of angels in disguise. We did not go back to his room. If we had, we probably would have found him crying. If there were tears, no doubt they were mingled with joy and gratitude.

I cannot take credit for this unusual caroling. It was my red-haired daughter who after dinner said, "Last year we went to the cancer hospice; tonight let's go to Arlington Hospital and sing for them," deftly brushing off all the hows and ifs and wherefores and firmly saying, "I'm sure they'll let us do it." And vans and cars soon drove off.

We are never alone. God is ever present to woo the sinner to Himself or to place a light on the pathway of His child. His Word tells us this. But what if we were that old gentleman in the hospital bed with no comfort of family or friends? Who would come at the end of Christmas day to let us conduct again, to share the hope of the season, to display God's mercy and grace?

I'll add a personal footnote. From the time our children were singing well, as soon as the tree was decorated we had a family carol sing around the tree almost every night—familiar carols, old carols, part songs, songs in French and German. We learned to harmonize, to sing all the parts, and to joyously improvise. As grandchildren were added, so also were added piano, violins, guitars, flute, and cello. Some nights it went on quite long—until someone said "Look at the clock!"

Someone will say, "But you are all so musical!" I have an idea that among the eleven men remaining with the Lord around that last Passover table several were not "musical." Yet for the final song of God's Son on earth in that upper room, eleven men sang a hymn with the Redeemer of the world.

Will God's song be heard in your family? Will it be heard often? If so, I am confident that, like a pebble dropping in a pool and creating endless ripples, it will not die. It will be heard over and over again, sometimes in ways you could never imagine.

What sweeter music can we bring
Than a carol, for to sing
The birth of this our heavenly King?
Awake the voice! Awake the string!
Heart, ear, and eye, and everything.

    Robert Herrick, 1591–1674

OUR BEST

Our family was in the final stages of our annual Christmas-tree decoration. First comes the snow, small amounts of granulated soap with a bit of warm water, stirred with an electric mixer to create small bowls of "snow." Then comes the ladling—everyone with a bowl—spoonful by spoonful, on top of each delicate branch. Then a fresh, moist batch, and repeat again and again. This process requires, of a meticulous father and four impatient little children, a half hour or more. After which—lo, a believable, snow-covered tree! There is no other way.

Now the icicles. No batches of slick tinsel or plastic icicles will do, but expensive, hand twisted glass or crystal icicles, purchased dearly, a few each year; but oh, how subtle and beautiful. Then come the old-fashioned globules, the ones with crusty decorations on colored glass. Finally, the children's special treasures. Each Christmas, on their gifts, tied into every bow, is an old-fashioned ornament of wood, glass, or straw. (When the children finish college, they'll take them with them to start their own tree.)

And so it was that particular Christmas. We had begun to congratulate ourselves on our decorated tree when we realized our young son was missing. In a moment he appeared. He had been in his room creating artwork with crayons and a sheet of 11x18-inch yellow newsprint (we kept quantities of it). He proudly held up his artistry—a picture, he said, of Santa. It was indeed a face. Some features were missing, but it had a beard and a tasseled hat.

My artistic soul began to shiver as he announced we should pin it on the tree. He said that when Santa entered the door (we had no fireplace) he would see it and think it was a mirror. My wife, my guardian angel, looked at me and sensed what would be coming. As I took a deep breath to respond, she poked me hard in the ribs. I let out my breath, standing silent and chastened.

Yes, Santa stayed pinned on our beautiful tree. The jolt to the ribs stopped me from doing what I was going to do. But it jolted more than the ribs, and that is the point of this story. I would have much time to reflect on the fact that I had not been a loving and caring father. My son had lived his few years in the middle of the arts. This Christmas he had produced for his family his very best, his most beautiful. But I had not encouraged him.

Shift of scene but not of subject. Not every director and his choir can perform music like *Messiah*, but all can choose what is beautiful and scriptural to honor God and to build His church. I once ministered to a small congregation in the hills of West Virginia. The choir was well prepared by the music director, the local optometrist. We did simple but beautiful things, a good bit of unison, songs that had the pentatonic "Sacred Harp" sound that originated in those hills, plus arrangements of hymns familiar to the congregation. Their joy and concentration and desire were just as great as that of a large professional choir. Their enthusiasm in learning ways to enhance and expand their ministry for the Lord was a bright light throughout the weekend.

In my years of working with church choirs and church musicians in every part of the US, I have seen them rise to the challenge of learning "what is even better" and experiencing greater breadth and power in the use of their God-given gifts. God's Word admonishes us all to keep growing. The little boy who drew Santa on the yellow paper, sang all the way through the University and went through a top-ten law school on a scholarship. He is now a federal judge who sings with his sixteen-year-old son in the bass section of their church choir.

The commitment to keep learning and growing in our music or speech or art is not a separate, elegant room that closes its doors to the rest of our lives or to the lives of others. It is just one of the tall buttresses that support the beautiful cathedral of a genuine Christlike life.

THE UNFLAWED WITNESS

MUSIC'S POWER

It was a concert by the North Austrian Symphony in Vienna. Some in the audience were in tuxes and long dresses. (In Europe at that time it was understood that suits and very nice dresses were the minimum requirement for attendance at such a concert.) The program consisted of an overture and two concertos, one for violin and one for cello, a combination rarely heard in the US but not uncommon in Europe at that time. My memory of the musical details has left me, but I well remember my experience.

Once the program started, the audience hardly moved a muscle. There was silent, sober concentration on the music. Then I developed a tickle in my throat. No doubt you have had that experience at some time. Without a cough drop, with nowhere to go, you sit and strangle until you just have to cough. And so it was, and what then? Heads quickly turned with hard stares from a number of well-dressed Austrians. This unscheduled drama continued for a few moments until the tickle mercifully left. At last, attention in our section became focused again on the orchestra rather than on the embarrassed cougher.

That year was the celebration of Johann Strauss, the "Waltz King"; and the Austrian government had decreed that every symphony concert, no matter how profound, must include a Strauss piece. None was listed on the program. Obviously, it would be a Strauss "surprise" encore.

There was enthusiastic applause as soloist, conductor, and orchestra took their bows. The conductor finally returned alone to polite applause, and then—silence. It was as though the large audience was taking one giant breath of anticipation. There was another moment of silence. The maestro raised his baton, and the beautiful, slow, quiet introduction to *The Blue Danube* began. The collective sigh was almost audible. Now there was electric concentration. The introduction moved into those three memorable "pick up" eighth notes, and the waltz began.

At first it was an almost imperceptible movement, but then one, then two, then more and more bodies, including the very well upholstered, began to sway in unison left and right, until the entire audience, including old and young, were transported to the polished floor of some castle's giant ballroom with no thought of how they were looking or acting. Rows and rows in waves of upbeats and downbeats, and now smiles and laughter. We were no longer at the "symphony"; we were in the mirror room of the Schönbrunn Palace! Forget the concertos! The final, tumultuous standing ovation could have been for the German soccer team at the World Cup! And music did this!

I have worked with professional musicians all my adult life, and I have never heard any proclaim that music is emotionally inert. There is not always agreement as to how music communicates, but professionals are unanimous: music has power. Those who rise in the professional music world spend a lifetime of practice and performance seeking the most compelling ways to release that power to their listeners. For them, music is a living, breathing thing.

And who would deny that except those who wish to keep moral standards out of music? If music can move us, it can move us in good or bad directions. Better to have music inert than dynamic and capable of affecting us in ways subject to moral judgment. So music, corpse-like, is laid on the examination table and declared lifeless and harmless.

Tell that to the 200,000 townsfolk of Tallin, Estonia, who gathered in the giant amphitheater at the edge of the city at the command of their Russian occupiers. Their famous annual choral festival had been taken over by the communists as a propaganda ploy. But when the required marches with Russian banners and the patriotic songs to Lenin and the "people" had ended, the choir of more than 8,000 spontaneously began to sing, without conductor, their beloved Estonian choral anthem.

Then the audience joined in. Now there were 200,000 voices, with a sound so great it drowned out the brass bands the Russians hastily put in place. It was credited as the power that brought about Estonia's successful "bloodless revolution."

We Christians can learn from the professionals. We can learn from the Estonian lay folk. Our music is a God-ordained, designated part of the worship and praise of the Creator. It is a means of testimony to the world and an encouragement to the believer. It has the power to serve worthy ends, and ends not worthy also.

PRAISING GOD

Those of us whose lot has been cast in the arts—performers, artists, teachers, conductors and composers—well know both the exhilaration and the demands that the arts produce. The concert hall can be an exciting place, but the practice room is often lonely and demanding. Always in front of us are high artistic goals and the example of those in our field who have reached them. For many the journey is daunting but successful. For a few it appears almost effortless. Others fall by the wayside.

In the world of the arts, the pressure on the individual is great as he measures himself against others and their achievements. Without genuine joy in his work and without some sense of accomplishment, he may find himself on a fruitless path. But there is a far better way for the Christian artist, genuinely glorious and forever satisfying.

The secular world measures success by talent and achievement. Its judgments are often right but are sometimes wrong. Even some of those most highly regarded by posterity have been misjudged in their time. See J. S. Bach in his final position as music director for the St. Thomas Church in Leipzig, with hundreds of compositions already behind him and still writing furiously (his output would eventually include over three hundred cantatas alone). He is preparing music for choir and instruments for every Sunday, providing the daily education of his school of choir boys, and is still writing. Though he is noted as a fine organist and a conscientious musical craftsman, several of his musical contemporaries are more highly regarded as composers. Even one son will be more highly esteemed in those times.

History, not current reputation, has finally determined the true value of J. S. Bach.

Bach now stands as possibly the greatest of the great composers. But Bach is also among the few who acknowledged faith in Christ alone. He left no doubt about it. On his completed manuscripts he often penned, *Soli Deo Gloria* (To God Alone Be the Glory).

This epigraph of Bach is the glorious path for the Christian artist. It is a path not always marked by public acclaim and earthly honors. It can be and sometimes is, but Christ Himself told us that it could be difficult, even dangerous. How then can this path be glorious? How can it warrant the hallmark of Bach's compositions?

This hallmark is not produced by any God-given talent we may have. It must be woven as a fine thread into the very cloth of our lives. Our faith cannot be a mere appendage to our goal-driven lives. It is vital in every part of our lives, central to all. The idea is found in Paul's marvelous statement to the Philippians, "For to me to live is Christ, and to die is gain" (Phil. 1:21).

> Thus, all my toilsome way along,
> I sing aloud Thy praises,
> That men may hear the joyful song
> My voice unwearied raises,
> Be joyful in the Lord, my heart,
> Both soul and body bear your part:
> To God all praise and glory.

> Johann J. Schütz, 1640–1690

> Translated by Frances E. Cox, 1812–1897

PLEASING GOD

A Latin phrase from Tinctoris, a fifteenth-century Flemish theorist, is lettered on the inside of the lid of my University's beautiful harpsichord [see figures 1 and 2]. *Deo delectare, dei laudes decorare* translates as "To please God and to decorate the praise of God." That sums it all up for those of us who are redeemed and who devote time and God-given talent to the creation and presentation of our art.

How easy it is to embrace the decorating part. Adornment is what the artist in us is born to do. But what about the part of pleasing God? Satan whispers, "Success in your art is essential to life satisfaction. Please yourself. Apply yourself totally to your art." The Christian should know better. Life satisfaction is in pleasing a person, Christ, the Son of God.

In the professional world have been persons of great talent who were very good at decorating, but that was about all. Their lives were full of their art, but their souls were empty. Without their art they would have had nothing. The Christian artist strives to excel in his decorating, but as part of a larger purpose. He seeks above all to please his God.

The Christian artist can never give himself to his art as entirely as the secular artist can. Artistic ego may rebel against this truth. It may cause him to make pragmatic choices against his Biblical conscience, afraid for his career. The saints of Hebrews 11 would not do so. They chose to walk a single path with God and often suffered for it.

Must we then live our lives under a shadow of pain and suffering? Not so. We live our lives under the shadow of the cross but also in the brilliance of the empty tomb and our risen Savior.

The world cannot understand our choice, but it will marvel at the love of Christ as it shines from our lives unaffected by artistic success or failure.

You may know someone who has realized both parts of Tinctoris's motto, to please God and adorn the praise of God. That person rides above the storm of petty envy and competition for acceptance. He lives and works as an artist at the highest level of his craft. No one can question his standards or the quality of his art. But that is not all about him or even the main part. He has a living, glowing testimony that cannot be demeaned or dimmed. His career is living proof of the victorious Christian life, a proof that puts to silence the critics' cynicism. And more important, that artist is loved by God's people and he loves them.

His choice, to please God above all, astounds an unbelieving world. Most astounding is that this choice has cost the Christian artist nothing he finally cares about. He has in fact acquired the ultimate satisfaction, the pleasure that comes from pleasing God.

FIGURE 1. Inside the lid of the Bob Jones University harpsichord

FIGURE 2. The Bob Jones University harpsichord

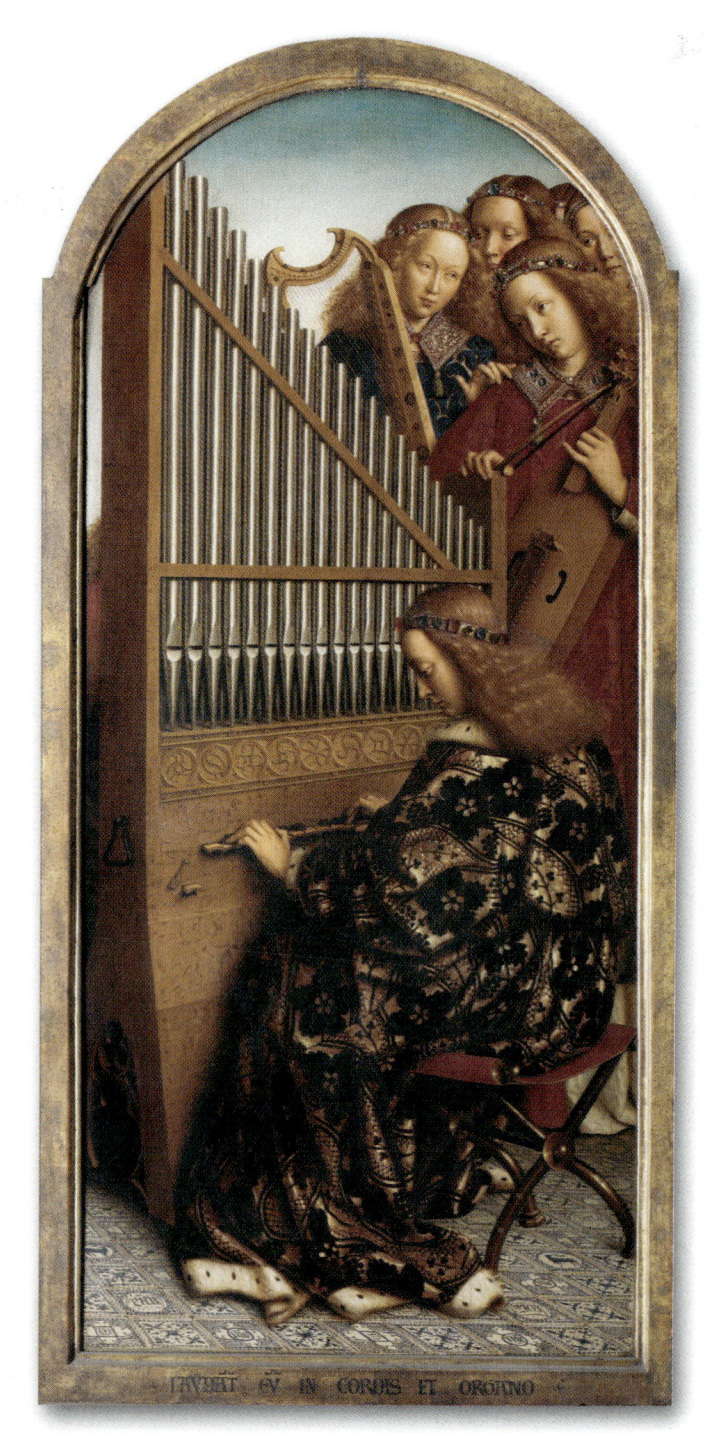

FIGURE 3. Angel musicians from the Ghent Altarpiece

FIGURE 4. Mary's jeweled neckline from the Ghent Altarpiece

FIGURE 5. The crucified Christ from the exterior of the Isenheim Altarpiece

FIGURE 6. The resurrection of Christ from the right wing of the Isenheim Altarpiece

FIGURE 7. Mirabel Palace and garden

FIGURE 8. Benjamin West's *The Ascension* on display in the War Memorial Chapel at Bob Jones University

FIGURE 9. Benjamin West's *Isaiah's Lips Anointed with Fire* on display in the War Memorial Chapel at Bob Jones University

FIGURE 10. Dr. Dwight Gustafson conducting in 2010

BEAUTY AND HOLINESS

In today's world the ideas of beauty and holiness seem far apart. Beauty may not be reachable in any ultimate sense, but it is still a goal for the artist, the composer, the performer, and the writer, as it has been for centuries. For them and others who share their values, holiness is considered only an ideal existing in the minds of intensely religious ascetics. Beauty is sought after, but holiness, though revered, is ignored.

Among Christian brethren the reverse is often the case. Holiness is sought after whereas beauty, though revered, gets ignored. The emphasis on holiness is understandable. The Old Testament proclaims holiness as God's principal attribute. In the New Testament the believer is urged to seek a life of holiness, described in Paul's Epistles as the finest testimony of a life in Christ separated to God. But the separation of these great values among Christians as well as among persons of the arts, though for different reasons, is unfortunate.

Goethe's great tragic poem-drama *Faustus* has been the inspiration for several major musical works. I have conducted the best of the Faust operas—Gounod's *Faust* and Boito's *Mefistofele*. Boito's opera follows the design of Goethe's drama quite closely. Boito was a writer and poet as well as a composer and thus was sensitive to the deliberate fashioning of Goethe's opening scene. There Satan brashly bargains with God for Faust's soul (much as in the book of Job) as galaxies swirl and heavenly choirs praise the Almighty. Gounod omits this.

Gounod's opening scene shows the aged philosopher in his study. Weary of his search for truth and beauty, he is confronted by Satan, disguised as a dashing Cavalier. Faust is offered the temporary return of youth with its ardor and passion on the condition that he put his eternal destiny in Satan's hands. He agrees, and the two close the scene with a bright lyric duet that speaks of youth, passion, and fulfillment of desire. It is appealing drama and music, but it avoids the core issue of Goethe's drama.

In the fall of 1969 the New York City Opera presented an exciting new production of *Mefistofele,* the first in forty years in the city. It was highly acclaimed. The title role was taken by Norman Treigle, possibly the finest actor-bass in opera at that time. Treigle said of the opera, "God, initially and finally, is the hero." Because it was on our "possibility" list I went to see it.

Some years later our plans for it went forward. When we began searching for singers, one of the major New York Artist managements contacted us. City opera was about to revive their fabled production, and a young bass was scheduled to make his New York debut. Would we be interested in his doing the role here as an "out of town" opening? And so it was that I conducted *Mefistofele* with young Samuel Ramey on his way to becoming the world's leading operatic basso [see fig. 10]. A number of years later, when we produced the opera a second time, the title role was sung by one of the world's greatest basses, noted earlier, Jerome Hines. Satan has occasionally sung well here, but only in opera!

Boito's Faust is, like Gounod's, the aged, despairing philosopher, but his desire, though it breeds sensuality, has much deeper roots. Before signing the contract with Satan he sings, "Se avvien ch'io dica all'attimo fuggente: Arrestati sei bello! allor ch'io muoia e m'inghiotta l'averno." "If it should ever happen that I say to the fleeting moment, 'Stay! for you are beautiful,' then I will forfeit my life, and Hell may devour me." That search for the ideal, that ultimate "beautiful moment" of supreme satisfaction, has been a driving force in the lives of many an artist, musician, and writer, as in many other lives as well. Some, like Faust, have sold their souls in an attempt to find it.

As I have stood behind the curtain at the end of operas and concerts, watching soloists take their bows before we entered together for the final bow, I occasionally have observed in them a desperate eagerness to walk into the spotlight and the applause, a desire to verify that the performance had achieved Faust's elusive moment of supreme beauty. But when the audience had gone and the hall was empty, when the make-up had been removed and the overcoat was in hand, there came the realization that the ecstasy had not materialized. Mortality had clouded the "great moment."

There is only one source of perfect beauty, Almighty God. His creation allows a glimpse of it, from the billions of microscopic strands of DNA to the billions of galaxies that soar through uncharted space, to the very light in which we live that still withholds the secret of its energy from modern science. We are dazzled and stand in awe. There is no question as to its beauty. But its Creator also said, "It is good."

Someday, as His redeemed ones, we will indeed stand in a beautiful, perfect place. We will join the multitudes of heaven proclaiming "Blessing, and honor, and glory, and power, be unto him that sitteth upon the throne, and unto the Lamb for ever and ever" (Revelation 5:13). Then, for the first time, we will see God's holiness ablaze in its ultimate beauty.

BENEDICTION

Let us find a place within the congregation looking on as King David, the Psalmist, stands before the tent that will be the first resting place for the ark of God. Now we hear him sing, "Give unto the Lord the glory due unto his name: bring an offering and come before him; worship the Lord in the beauty of holiness" (1 Chronicles 16:29). It is God's beauty and God's holiness. It is beyond human comprehension. Someday, as we enter eternity, we will for the first time look upon that holy beauty. For now we must content ourselves with traces of that beauty in human art it has inspired.

We who work with choral and solo music often recall, almost instantaneously, a section of Scripture or a hymn text when we think of a beautiful musical moment, or vice versa. I can remember this happening in our home. Someone would quote Scripture or a line from a song, and my wife would begin to sing!

The beautiful benediction at the end of Moses' great song about God, Psalm 90, is such a text for me. I have conducted the Ralph Vaughan Williams setting of the Psalm and the more rugged and unyielding setting by the American composer, Charles Ives. Both are beautiful and powerful, but somehow the Ives piece, with its powerful climaxes and unexpected changes, rising in intensity as the Psalmist moves through his description of the timeless God in all circumstances and then the weakness and demise of mortal life, all somewhat like an angry, changeable sea, prepares us best for the contemplation of one of Scripture's most beautiful benedictions.

Ives had written and rewritten the piece for over thirty years. As a layman and a serious composer, he was little respected and almost unknown. His wife recalls his saying that it was the only one of his works he was satisfied with.

The ideal place for us to perform it was our War Memorial Chapel, where eight monumental paintings of biblical scenes by the eighteenth-century court painter Benjamin West seem to reverberate solemnly with the music [see figures 8 and 9]. When the rugged music subsides, we are left with a serene choral setting over slowly rocking C naturals in the organ pedals as the choir begins the benediction, almost like a chorale: "So teach us to number our days, that we may apply our hearts unto wisdom." A solo voice intones "Return, O Lord, how long? And let it repent Thee concerning Thy servants."

Then from three hidden locations in the chapel comes the sound of church bells, notated to sound as random and natural as possible, as you would hear them at evensong in a small New England town. Under the bells and over the slow, rocking pedal C of the organ the choir continues simply:

O satisfy us early with thy mercy; that we may rejoice and be glad all our days.
Make us glad according to the days wherein Thou hast afflicted us, and the years wherein we have seen evil.
Let Thy work appear unto Thy servants, and Thy glory unto their children.

Then, with the bells still sounding and the choir in longer notes, so soft they are almost speaking, comes the great moment.

And let the beauty of the Lord our God be upon us: and establish
Thou the work of our hands upon us;
Yea, the work of our hands establish Thou it. Amen.

Beauty and holiness: the beauty of our God upon us, our separation to Him in all of life, and the establishing of the work of our hands by His blessing—this is ultimate beauty for the Christian, a beauty in which holiness is celebrated and not diminished or ignored.

CODA

HIS GLORY

I hope our conversations have been pleasant and helpful. I hope they have given you a scriptural, real-life view of God's working in the lives, families, and careers of Christians in the arts. Most of all, I pray that God will use them to stimulate and guide your thinking as you seek God's way in your life. Like all good conversations, even after the coffee cups are empty and we head toward the door, we are still talking, summing up or enlarging on our discussion. That in fact is what this final conversation is. In music it is called a coda, a distinct closing section that sums up the main themes but that may also add some new material.

If these articles have met their purpose, they have summoned us, in practical ways, to what I have called the brighter witness, the reach for excellence by Christians of all ages—and all sizes! God has given us individual personalities with diverse abilities. We are as varied as snowflakes. We should be as pure and beautiful as they are. We should strive for their perfection. The Creator's work is to be emulated there.

Whether it has been a choir in a small country church, an all-state Christian high-school choir, or a large adult chorus singing "Achieved Is the Glorious Work" from Haydn's *Creation,* I have observed God's people rising to the challenge of doing the most beautiful performance conceivably to be asked of them, and endeavoring to do it just a little better than that, just a little more beautifully, for the glory of God.

Too often we become satisfied with normal, with well enough is good enough. The pursuit of excellence seems too taxing a path. And yet the ascent to our best is a God-honored, beautiful path. Why should one aim merely at where he happens to be presently and seek to go no further?

The world beckons in all our decision making, not least in our choices in the arts. Immediate mass communication has determined for us what is normal and acceptable by mass vote, not by any predetermined standard. Quality and value have been replaced by popularity, by average taste which had already become trivial and banal when the digital revolution began. What once was ugly now passes by without comment, let alone protest. Discrimination has been swept aside by desire.

Unfortunately, technology has opened family doors to every aspect of today's popular culture. Driven by near omnipresent digital images, technology is gradually skewing our sense of values, Christian as well as secular. What has genuine value? What is worthy of enjoyment? What is worthy of contemplation? Children especially are affected. The home should be a place where the beautiful is daily present and loved and cherished, where wise decisions are valued and not scorned. Too frequently it is not.

I have a special concern for Christian families with talented children. Families do not often enter discussions of the arts, but they are the God-given primary force in shaping young lives. Unfortunately in some Christian families there is no earnest attempt to tie God-given talent to spiritual development and testimony. Children often do not experience the joy of serving God with their family in line with their own gifts. Family, career, and Christian witness are not separate worlds. They should be joined as one in God's plan for our lives.

The opening paragraph of the apostle Paul's letter to the Philippians has been a guiding beacon for me on these issues. Verses 9 through 11 provide clear direction for every believer in every age.

> And this I pray, that your love may abound yet more and more in knowledge and in all judgment; that ye may approve things that are excellent; that ye may be sincere and without offence till the day of Christ;

being filled with the fruits of righteousness, which are by Jesus Christ unto the glory and praise of God.

We conclude from this passage that spiritual choices, whether in our recreational use of the arts, or between worship styles, or among career options, all spring from an abounding love for Christ, a love that encompasses every part of our lives.

This love embraces the knowledge we gain—and we are here admonished to gain knowledge, to be knowledgeable. A useful Christian does not live in an intellectual vacuum. He is ever a learner. Such a love directs the Christian's judgment, his discernment. He seeks God's best in his life, and therefore for him values are important. Indeed, he seeks excellence. It is not enough for him that his efforts carry him only to what is normal or popular or convenient by general worldly standards. He does not congratulate the trivial. The bar is raised high for his life because he is driven by his love for Christ and Christ's love is in control. These divine standards produce their own proof: sincerity without offence, the fruits of righteousness by Jesus Christ, the glory and praise of God.

Notice that whereas the passage begins with what governs our choices, Christ's love, it finishes with God's glory, with that brighter witness which is the overarching theme of this book. It should be clear by now that the brighter witness does not come about as the result of our efforts. God must light the fire, a truth never to be forgotten. But we do have a part, and the result can be immensely satisfying. In the arts, as in our other undertakings, what God has struck aglow will flame beautifully when a love for Him and a concern for His glory blaze on the altar of our lives.

PHOTO CREDITS

Figures 1 & 2. Bob Jones University Harpsichord, © 2012, BJU Photo Services

Figure 3. Angel musicians with St. Cecilia, from the Ghent Altarpiece, 1432 (oil on panel) detail, Eyck, Hubert (c.1370-1426) & Jan van (1390-1441) / St. Bavo Cathedral, Ghent, Belgium / © Lukas - Art in Flanders VZW / Photo: Hugo Maertens / The Bridgeman Art Library

Figure 4. Detail of the Virgin Mary, from the Ghent Altarpiece, 1432 (oil on panel), Eyck, Hubert (c.1370-1426) & Jan van (1390-1441) / St. Bavo Cathedral, Ghent, Belgium / © Lukas - Art in Flanders VZW / Photo: Hugo Maertens / The Bridgeman Art Library

Figure 5. The Isenheim Altarpiece, c.1512-15 (oil on panel), Grunewald, Matthias (Mathis Nithart Gothart) (c.1480-1528) / Musee d'Unterlinden, Colmar, France / The Bridgeman Art Library

Figure 6. The Resurrection of Christ, from the right wing of the Isenheim Altarpiece, c.1512-16 (oil on panel) detail, Grunewald, Matthias (Mathis Nithart Gothart) (c.1480-1528) / Musee d'Unterlinden, Colmar, France / Giraudon / The Bridgeman Art Library

Figure 7. Mirabel Palace and garden, gary718/Shutterstock.com

Figure 8. *The Ascension*/Benjamin West, P.R.A./From the Bob Jones University Collection

Figure 9. *Isaiah's Lips Anointed with Fire*/Benjamin West, P.R.A./From the Bob Jones University Collection

Figure 10. Dr. Dwight Gustafson, © 2010, BJU Photo Services